DROPSHIPPING ARBITRAGE

HOW TO MAKE MONEY ONLINE & BUILD YOUR OWN ONLINE BUSINESS, ECOMMERCE, EBAY, AMAZON, SHOPIFY, AND PASSIVE INCOME

THOMAS CORDIER

All rights reserved. No part of this publication may be
reproduced, stored in a retrieval system, or transmitted in any form or by any means, electronic, mechanical,
photocopying or otherwise, without the prior permission of the copyright owner.

© Copyright 2018 by IF Publishing

interfigroup@gmail.com

Contents

Introduction

Chapter 1 — Five Golden Rules to Dropshipping

Chapter 2 — Reasons for Starting a Dropshipping Business

Chapter 3 — Things to Consider

Chapter 4 — The Advantages and Disadvantages

Chapter 5 — How to get Started

Chapter 6 — How to find a Reputable Dropshipping Supplier

Chapter 7 — Selling Through an eBay Store

Conclusion

Introduction

Dropshipping is a type of retailing where, instead of the retailer (meaning you) actually keeping the goods in stock at their own location, they instead pass the order, along with the shipment details from a customer, to a wholesaler. It is then the job of the wholesaler to dispatch the goods ordered directly to your customer for you. The great thing about this method is that not only do you not need to have a large warehouse for storing all the goods you are selling, but also you make a profit through the price you pay for it wholesale, and the price that you sell it to your customer for.

In fact, where dropshipping is concerned, you are actually acting as the middleman for the product that your customer receives and the manufacturer who produces it. This particular type of system is extremely beneficial to both small retail shops, as well as internet based stores, or those people who use mailing catalogs in order to generate sales for their companies. In fact, many customers who purchase their products in this way seem to not be too bothered that there is a delay between the time when the products are ordered and when they actually have them arrive.

But the biggest problem that is being addressed by dropshipping is that retailers no longer have to worry about controlling their inventory, as this is done for them by the wholesaler instead. Unfortunately, in a more traditional retail setting, the products a store owner orders will be ordered in bulk, and they will then need to be kept in a secure location until they can be displayed and sold. What this means is that you are adding costs to an already large budget, as you will need to have storage space available, along with hiring staff to maintain the storage area and ensure that the goods are ready for delivery to the store and to know what levels each product is at. You will also need to spend money investing in a good quality security system in order to prevent the goods from being stolen. However, if you were to use dropshipping instead, then you do not need to retain a large stock of your inventory on site, and also you no longer needed to employ a large team of staff.

Also, you will find that a large number of manufacturers now find the idea of dropshipping as a good investment, as it is also lowering their costs as well. Plus they are gaining an additional sales person who they do not actually pay a wage to. They are also saving themselves money as they no longer need to arrange for the delivery of large quantities of their goods to a retailer, so they are cutting down on their handling and fuel costs this way. Instead, they can use the more inexpensive shipping methods that are now readily available by using either UPS, FedEx or a locally based delivery company to ensure that their products are delivered directly to the customer. Plus, as many manufacturers have spent vast amounts of money ensuring that their warehouses are completely secure, they know that their products are safe until the day that they are dispatched, rather than them sitting in the back room of some retailer's shop with very little or no security on the property.

Yet there are some drawbacks to running a dropshipping business, and these we will look at in more detail later on in this book. Through this book, we will provide you with how you need to get started in the business of dropshipping, along with what you will need and the benefits, as well as the drawbacks.

Chapter 1 –

Five Golden Rules to Dropshipping

If you want to ensure that your dropshipping business is profitable, there are a number of things you need to remember. In this chapter, we will look more closely at these five golden rules to ensure that you can run a profitable business.

In order to make your business as profitable as possible, you need to find a product which will sell in sufficient quantities, as well as one which will provide you with a good mark up, in order for it to be truly profitable. Therefore, it is important that you try to determine what the demand for the product is, and also what competition, if any, there is for this particular product. Also, if you can, take a look at what your competition is charging for it. You may find that some businesses will have a much lower profit margin than others, including you.

It is best when first starting out selling products using dropshipping, that you only sell a select few. Plus, also that those that you do select are related, or can be targeted and sold to the same market set. It is important that you do not try to sell every dropshipping product that you find, as this will help you concentrate more on marketing your goods, as well as keeping your own costs to a minimum. Plus, you are more likely to make an impact in the market place as well.

Due to its increased popularity, it is important that you find a reputable dropshipper for your business. Unfortunately, over recent months there have been many scams that have come to light in this particular industry. Avoid those people who are offering to sell you lists of dropshippers for 100's of dollars, unfortunately many of these are middlemen who are posing as dropshippers themselves, and will then charge much more than you actually should be paying. Remember, the whole idea of using dropshipping is to keep your costs down rather than raising them, but also still be able to make a profit at the end of the day.

Also, if you are able to, avoid the "turnkey" internet businesses which are willing to sell you a package of products, e-commerce and marketing for an exorbitant membership fee or charge you a monthly fee. These types of businesses, you will soon find, do not actually help, but rather hinder, and you will soon find that you are not making any profit whatsoever, while they are.

However, do not let what we have written above frighten you off, instead just be aware of these pitfalls. However, one of the best ways of finding a reputable dropshipper is through looking at such directories as "Chris Malta's Worldwide Brands". This provides you with a whole list of legitimate, as well as reputable, dropshippers that you may wish consider using.

You will still need to deal with the problems associated with back orders and returns. Unfortunately, not all the hassles associated with running a normal retail business can be eliminated from a business that is run online. There will be times when you find that a product your customer has ordered is not in stock, and so will not be available for dispatch immediately. Therefore, you will need to work out these matters with your dropshipper ahead of any of these problems occurring. This will then provide you with answers that you can provide to your customer should such an event occur.

Finally, it is important that you treat your business just like any other business, so do not spam people. Also, do not use either a personal or free web page address for your online store, and also ensure that you register the business with your County Clerk. It is also important that you register with the Tax office so that you have a Tax ID number…and be prepared to file taxes each year.

As long as you start off by expecting that your business is going to make a decent profit, then the chances are that you will automatically see an increase in this.

Chapter 2 –

Reasons for Starting a Dropshipping Business

If you are looking for one of the best opportunities to be had today for running a business from home, and cost little if anything to set up, then a dropship business is probably the answer for you. Not only can you run this business from the comfort of your own home, you will not have to worry about keeping large amounts of inventory in stock and you will not have to worry about getting the products shipped to your customers. Plus, you can still run this type of business while working in your normal day to day job. However, if the business really does get off the ground, then you can become a work from home mom or dad instead.

In order to get your dropship business started, you will need either your own website, or you can sell your products on eBay. Then once an order is received and has been paid for by a customer, you send the order over to your dropship supplier and they then send the order directly to your customer while you still make a profit. Also, you will need to set up an electronic payment system such as those provide by PayPal.

If you were to carry out a search of the web today, you will be amazed at the number of people who are making money through a dropshipping business. There are even some who are actually earning a 6 figure salary from theirs, and others who are just doing it part time in order to earn a little extra cash to provide them with a better way of life. In fact, many people often start their dropshipping business as a part time business, and it is only after the business has really taken off do they decide to do it full time instead.

The great thing about setting up dropshipping business is you do not need any special skill sets in order to get it started. All it really needs is a person who is willing to dedicate their time to ensure that the business succeeds, as well as having a computer and this being connected to the internet.

But the first thing you need to do once you decide to set up a dropshipping business is to form a good relationship with your dropship supplier. Once this has been formed, then you can start selling their products online, either through your own website, or on one of the many auction sites such as eBay.

What you are actually doing is acting as a middleman and bringing together those who want to buy a particular product and those that are selling it, while still collecting a profit for you. The greatest benefit to be had from setting up this type of business is that you do not have to worry about inventory or paperwork as with a normal retail business, as this is all the worry of your dropship supplier instead.

The other great thing about setting up a dropshipping business is that you should find yourself almost making money instantly. If not today then tomorrow or the next day, but it certainly will not be long before you should start to see your first profits.

All you need to do is find a product that you feel people will buy, find a reputable dropship supplier, and then start advertising the product on eBay. By using this method, you will find it costs very little in order to get your business up and running.

However, as with any business, it is best that you ensure that the products you are supplying are of the best quality possible, and also provide the best customer service that you can. So if you are selling your products through an auction site, then make sure you keep in touch with what is happening. If any of your customers have a question, then make sure that you respond as quickly as possible and follow up afterwards to ensure that they are satisfied with the information you provided to them.

Also, always select products that there are not thousands of them selling on the internet. By doing this, your business will not only be much more fun, but will also be much more profitable. So before you start selling any products through a dropshipping business, you should do as much research as possible first. Look for those products which have not saturated the market, or that has very few people competing for the customers, and therefore, the sales.

But what you do need to remember is that starting a dropshipping business is very easy, and you can run it from anywhere, especially out of your own home. Also, such a business can be run from anywhere in the world, and will cost you very little in getting it started.

Chapter 3 –

Things to Consider

As you will soon discover, dropshipping is an extremely effective business model for anyone who wants to start an online retail business. You can either run it through your own website, or through some other outlet, such as an auction site.

However, because this form of online business has become so easy to do, and because of its increased popularity, many prospective dropshipping businesses have become targets for the less reputable people online, such as scammers.

Unfortunately, many people who do not really understand what dropshipping is about only see it as a way of getting rich quick. Because of this, there are plenty of people out there who are ready to exploit them. In this article, we will look more closely at the things you should consider before you decide to go ahead and set up a dropshipping business for yourself.

1. You need to carry out plenty of research with regard to dropship sources. It is best if you avoid using search engines when doing this, as they will also offer up a list of the less reputable companies around, as well as providing you with page upon page of links which are completely useless. However, once you have found a reputable source for the information that you require, and then the real work begins.

2. Avoid any companies which expect you to pay them an up front fee (membership or monthly). Also avoid those which offer you a fully featured dropshipping solution that provides you with a website and everything else that you need in order to get your business off the ground.

3. Ensure the dropshippers you are looking at require a valid wholesale certificate from you. You will gain this through a business license, so avoid any that don't have that requirement at all costs. Unfortunately, most of the companies which are willing to do business with an illegal business will usually be middlemen, who then send your order through to the wholesale company, and will end up taking a cut of the profits that you are trying to make.

The best way to find a legitimate dropshipping company is as follows:-

   a. If you have seen a product which you are interested in selling, then contact the company producing it direct. Enquire if they have a dropshipping facility, and if they don't, then they are likely to be a light bulk seller. This means that they will only normally sell their products wholesale with a minimum of say around $200 or so (in many cases, the minimum number is much higher).

    b.   Another way is looking at such directories that have been set up and deal directly with legitimate dropshipping companies only. One such directory is WorldWideBrands. Such directories offer you an extensive searchable list of products, and which companies supply them. So if you are looking for a way to save yourself time in searching for good quality products to sell through your online business, then these directories are certainly the right way to go.

4. However, once you have found a company that does offer dropshipping facilities, <u>you will need to get a valid reseller/wholesale certificate</u>. Yet, what the exact requirements are in order for you to obtain this certificate will vary from state to state. But the minimum requirement for starting any dropshipping business online is that you have a business license.

5. Now you need to contact the dropshipping company in question and set up an account with them. Unfortunately, you may find that because your business is new, and you are not able to supply any references, then you may find that you need to set up a pre-paid account with them. Normally, this means that they will charge your purchases to a credit card instead of providing you with a line of credit. In order for this to be done, you will need to fill out a credit card form, an account application and provide them with your wholesale certificate. Once this has been received, they will then provide you with a wholesale catalog and anything else that you need in order to get your business up and running with their products.

6. Also, do not be fooled by those sites offering you a dropship directory for a fee (normally around $5 to $15). Unfortunately, these are normally copies of the more legitimate lists provided by reputable directories, and will often be out of date. So really, you are better off going to one of the more reputable directories and paying them a little extra in order to get a regularly updated list.

7. Now that you have found the product which you are interested in selling, and you have made arrangements with the dropshipper in question, it is time to get your site up and running, or your account set up with one of the more reputable auction sites, such as eBay.

Chapter 4 –

The Advantages and Disadvantages

Although dropshipping today is a very hot topic being discussed among many retailers, and it does have many benefits, it may not be the best option for every business. However, in this chapter we will take a closer look at some of the advantages, as well as disadvantages to be had from running an online dropshipping business.

First, if you are just starting out in setting up an online business, and do not have much operating capital, then this may be the best option for you to go with. The great thing about this particular type of business is that you do not need to hold vast stocks of the products that you are selling. Instead, this is all done for you by the dropshipping supplier you have gone into partnership with. This results in you eliminating a significant cost in order for your business to be set up and to get it running.

The site you set up can be produced very quickly, and so be providing the product to those people you are targeting.

As you are getting the customers orders before you actually order the goods from the supplier, this means that you have little or no initial investment to make.

Because you are not actually holding any of the inventories yourself, then you do not need to pay either for storage facilities, or having to invest in expensive merchandise which you may not in fact sell.

Setting up an online dropshipping business provides you with the chance to diversify what you are actually offering to your customers. In fact, you will only be limited by not being able to find the right dropshipper for the product or items that you wish to sell.

Although there are plenty of advantages to setting up a dropshipping business, there are many disadvantages as well.

First, as you do not own the inventory that you are selling, then you will usually find that you have no control on how the product is packaged. Also, you will not be able to include any coupons or offers in to the package which can help in increasing the amount of return business you get.

Every company which offers their dropshipping services will have a different fee structure, so carry out as much in depth research as possible. In fact, you do not want to end up with high shipping costs, as this will only make people less reluctant to purchase their goods from you.

With dropshipping, because you are only ordering one item at the time rather than bulk amounts, then you will not expect to get the same kinds of discounts.

If you decide to sell multiple products that are supplied by multiple dropshipping companies, then you will also see a significant increase in the fees that you pay to the dropshippers, which, in turn, will need to be passed onto your customer in order for you to make a profit.

There are many suppliers who will be able to provide you with dropshipping services that you can use to integrate their products into your website. However, you may find that you will be charged a fee for using a particular service through them, so be sure that you carry out your research thoroughly before opting for one particular dropship supplier.

One major drawback to be had from setting up a dropshipping business is that not all manufacturers allow for dropshipping. This is because they will need to employ more staff (extra costs) in order for them to process these individual orders, and could result in delays in their normal shipping and receiving system. There are other companies who will only supply in bulk, so this means that it is impossible for smaller outlets to get custom orders provided for them for select numbers of items.

However, when dropshipping is available, certainly many small as well as internet based businesses find that it can solve many more problems than those it may create.

Chapter 5 –

How to get Started

It really is very easy to get your dropshipping business up and running. The main pieces of equipment that you will need are a good computer, and also a good quality internet connection.

But not only is it fairly easy to get your business up and running, you will find that there are very few barriers which will prevent you from getting started, and the cost for starting out is very low, so you should not need to invest much money up front initially.

However, below these are the steps that you will need to take in order to get your dropshipping business up and running.

1. Set yourself up an online shop, either using one of the many online shop builder programs available, or by building your own site, or setting up an account with an auction site such as eBay (if you choose to use eBay as your primary selling place, I recommend getting a good auction template that you can simply plug your information into to save time).

2. Find your wholesale supplier who has the product that are looking to sell, and who offers a dropshipping service.

3. Once you have found the company that you want to deal with, you can open an account with them.

4. Next thing you need to do is start building your site, using both content and images that the dropshipping supplier has provided, or that you have produced yourself (I recommend the latter, as it will distinguish you from other sellers who may be utilizing the same dropshipper).

5. Set up a system on your site so that you know when an order has been placed for a particular item, and so payment can be taken.

6. Pass on the details of the order directly to your dropshipping supplier. Once they receive the order, they will then bill you at the price that you have both agreed upon, and then they will arrange for the item to be dispatched. In most cases, the dropshipping supplier will provide labels which refer to the business or website where the order has come from, rather than from their own business.

Chapter 6 –

How to Find a Reputable Dropshipping Supplier

Probably one of the best ways of finding a reputable dropshipping supplier is through contacting the wholesalers direct, and asking if they operate a dropshipping service.

However, the other way you can find details regarding reputable dropshipping suppliers is through the internet, and this is probably much easier than having to ring round hundreds of different wholesalers.

First, the best thing you can do is search the internet using the terms "drop shipping", "dropshipping", "drop ship" or "dropship" and include with this the product that you are interested in. Normally by doing this, you will find the results that you get are pretty good.

Also, take a look at some of the sponsored links that you find in the results search pages that are offered up by such sites as Google and Yahoo. These will often give you a good idea of some of the more up to date dropshippers that are around.

Join a dropshipping forum, and there you will be able to chat to many like minded people who can provide you with details and information on the best dropshippers for a product that you are particularly interested in.

Then there are dropshipping directories. These are probably the easiest way of all for finding dropshippers. However, it is important that you only use the more reputable ones such as WorldWideBrands or Drop Ship Source Directory.
Even though you may have found a good dropshipping company, one of the biggest barriers you may find is the cost. There are some companies which will charge you a monthly membership fee costing hundreds of dollars, and there are others which require you to have a business license before you can apply for membership.

Also, there are many people around who think that dropshipping is a scam, and this is simply not true. Again, there are a few companies who are willing to exploit us, but these are in the minority rather than the majority. If you were to look closely at this subject, you will find that more than 1.1 million people around the world have been able to utilize dropshipping effectively in order to earn an income.

Also, you may be one of the lucky ones who finds a company that does not want any up front fees in order for you to get started.

Chapter 7 –

Selling through an eBay Store

You will soon be surprised at just how many sellers there are on auction sites, such as eBay, who use dropshipping in order to earn an income.

Certainly, if you are looking for a good way of gaining experience when selling online, it is by setting up an eBay account. The great thing is that you will have millions of potential customers who may well be interested in your products. In this chapter, we look at just what you need to do in order to get your dropshipping business up and running on an auction site such as eBay.

As previously discussed in other chapters of this book, you need to find yourself a reputable and reliable wholesale company that also provides a dropshipping service. Also, choose products from the wholesale company that are not already abundantly available online. Once you have found your wholesale company, you then need to find out about their dropshipping program, along with the fees that they charge for this service, and how they handle both the payments that you make to them, and the way in which the products are shipped. Then, once you are satisfied with what they are providing, and you have got your account set up with them, now you can move on to the next stage, which is signing up to the auction site of your choice and get ready to start selling.

When you sign up to an auction site, you are now able to start selling the products you have available through their auctions. When setting up an auction item, you should ask your dropshipper to provide you with stock images that you can use, along with descriptions of the items in question. It is important, though, that any items you are selling are placed into the correct category, and that you carry out as much research with regard to the price of them compared to what your competitors may be offering them at. It is also important that the description you provide helps it stand out from that of your competitors. A great way of doing this is by looking at a few of the power sellers on these auction sites, what they have and how they have set them up. Also, never price your products too low at the start of the auction, as you will need to factor in fees for posting the items, as well as ensuring that you making some profit on it yourself. Certainly, if you find that the winning bid is much lower than you expected, you can soon find yourself losing money rather than making it. So carrying out research with regard to the product you are selling is very important before you start posting any items.

But if you want, rather than just selling the items through an auction, you can set yourself up with a store, such as an eBay store. This can certainly be more cost effective because the fee for listing items in this way is much more affordable. However, one disadvantage to this method is that your store may not get the same sort of exposure as an item that you have put up for auction. But if you are really clever, then you can utilize both of these methods in order to bring more customers to you.

But what is really important if you do decide to use this route for selling products from a dropshipping business, is that you provide a good customer service facility, as well as quick shipping. Soon you will find that by being able to provide a quality service, these customers will return time and again to purchase from you.

Also, eBay has a great email marketing feature, which means that you are able to email all your repeat customers who have decided to opt in to your email list with just one click on the mouse.

So as you can see from above, setting up a dropshipping business using an auction site such as eBay can be very painless indeed. However, <u>it is vital that you research your product thoroughly,</u> as well as finding a reliable and reputable dropship supplier.

Conclusion

As you can see from above, setting up a dropshipping business is an excellent way to get started with an online business, and if done correctly, should not be an expensive project.

As you will soon discover, there are hundreds of companies who are willing to provide dropship products to you. Whether it is gifts of items for the home, to power tools and furniture, the choices are immense.

Certainly, dropshipping will offer you many advantages if you are only starting up an online business with very little or no capital. One of the main ones being that the product you are selling does not need to be paid for until it is actually sold, and as you are paid for it by the customer, then the outlay you make to the dropshipper supplier is nothing. Along with not having to make any outlay to the supplier in order for the product to be sold on your site, you also do not have to worry about storage and handling costs, as this is all covered for you by the dropship supplier you are using.

Plus, by setting up a site where your goods are supplied to you by a dropship supplier, you can offer a much wider variety of items, from a number of different suppliers, and your customers will never know any different.

Unfortunately, there are some downsides to running a dropshipping business, and the main ones are that you do not have any control over the inventory management, whether the product is readily available and if the orders can be fulfilled and shipped on time to the customer who has ordered them.

But if you are still interested in setting up a dropshipping business in order to earn an extra income online, then carry out as much research as possible.

The best thing of all is that, when setting up such a business, it does not need to be expensive or time consuming.

Printed in the USA
CPSIA information can be obtained
at www.ICGtesting.com
LVHW082319290424
778848LV00038B/2015